You, Who Creates

Daniel Viragh

Published by West End Media
PO Box 99140 Davie PO
Vancouver, British Columbia
V6G 0B7
Canada

Book designed by Laurenthia Sugianto.
Cover art by Laurence Patenaude.
Author drawing by Mr. Sugihara (Fukui, Japan).

For Edit

The poems presented here are offerings to the community.
I have done my best to polish them, so that they might convey
their message as accurately as possible.

The poems exist in themselves: they speak best when left alone.
Some are more intimate than others. Some treat sensitive topics
like trauma. Others aspire to convey various physiological states
 and wants.

Please, walk carefully. Not all poems will appeal to everyone.

The poems chronicle a certain process of healing. Sometimes
healing involves re-experiencing or facing difficult memories.
I encourage you to discuss the words with people in your midst.

Blessings and thanks,

Daniel Viragh.

Acknowledgements

I am extremely grateful to my Vancouver-based therapist.

I would like to thank the few family members whose support over the past three years have rendered this work possible and worthwhile: Edit Fazakas, Dóra Pataricza and Christina Viragh. Thanks as well to Orad Reshef, Tal Grebel-Avihai, Leibish Hundert, and Elysée Wilson-Egolf for their support in the darkest of times. This book would not have been possible without my daily yoga practice, and without the spiritual companionship of the yogis whom I've met, both at the Sivananda Ashram in Val-Morin, Quebec, and at KarmaTeachers Centre for Yoga and Meditation in Vancouver.

And finally I would like to thank Laurenthia Sugianto for designing this beautiful volume and the amazing website to accompany to it.

Table of Contents

Please Help

There's really nothing to say
I'm dying and — it's beyond terrible!
The syringes are late
They're gonna metabolize me
Feed me morphine and ibuprofen
and lotus-leaf root and
gingko biloba and
balsamic vinegar.

Please help
I'm in room 1105
Down the hall from me
An old man is coughing
Some teenagers are experimenting
by bringing their beds close
together.

When I take myself
seriously, I have
severe depression and
anxiety;
when I don't,
I have nothing to say.

I'm in room 1105
You'll find the key under my
washbasin
My phylacteries are there too
Help yourself to my occult cornucopia
of religious taboos.

I've repeatedly emphasized to my doctors
My desire to be humane
As they murder and I steal
And we diagnose fear and shame
as loving and longing
for that which was lost,
a recess of the reason
while the spirit evolves.

Tell me, O druids of mercy,
If I'm wed to my solitude
And my guilt is displaced
Is it really as easy
As the two kids next door?

Rest

He's not coming here
He'll never see this place
His judgments are over
His voice has been erased

There's no need to go now
You're not alone

From your persecutions, now rest
Breathe — you've been blessed
Take this space — it's yours —
You're no one's guest

We still love you
You're not alone

You, Who Creates

You, who creates
the ashes and the dusk
Behold the flame
that struggles as it must
Give us
of your glory
Holy are we
Only with your trust.

I yearn to mourn
the fragments of the past
I strive to speak
but I know my words come last.
How then
to capture beauty?
Holy, holy
Ye who serve and pass.

My country, it has no borders;
My soul, no boundaries on earth.
These rocks are my only pillow;
My staff, the only thing I'm worth.
So pray as one;
And comfort all;
Then say with me:
Amen.

These Words

These words that I perpetuate,
from their meaning I can't hide.
I thought I'd be a waffle,
or a snake; instead I became a guide:

A seeker of refuge, a carrier of weight,
a trader in instances, a necrologist, a gate
through which
my entrails are to be trampled,
my lunacy exposed,
my idealism embittered,
my fallacies deposed.

I did not ask for words;
they begat the me and we.
Let us rejoice in their concert,
and pronounce an end to hostility.

Physical

I'm not gonna lie.
It'd be nice if I still had your phone number.

Lost Wedding Band

While walking to work
on Thursday morning,
my ring
must have slipped off
my finger in the rain.
Please,
if you find it,
call me —
or my husband.

Look At Me Now

Look at me now:
You think that's gold you're wearing?
You think that silver pendant is real?
You think the sky's really there?
That drinking involves anything
but the universe displacing itself?
There's no molecule in you
that isn't pure: why besmirch the vase?
Why mask the nave?
Yours is a special type of evil,
that hurts without purpose.

I Still Remember

I still remember
when I stroked your chest
when you held me close, when your glasses fell.

I still remember
when you held the pen
when I formed the letters "A" and "men".

I still remember
when you bathed me clear
when you stroked my hair, called me dear.

I still remember
when you read me from your book
when you gave me a stick, when we crossed the brook.

I still remember
when you made us soup
when you borrowed a ladle, when we had no roof.

And I still remember
when you held my hand
when our mother died, you helped us stand.

Creation

Must you die a little
every time that you create?
Why is yearning so brittle?
Why does my world still hate?
Can you understand the reticules of time?
The shades and hues and melon dews
of earth and sky and crime?

The messengers of evil,
do they also die at dawn?
Will everything be peaceful
once my infant son is grown?
And what about you, the poet,
Thou usurper of the throne:
will you help us seek the lovely,
the manifold, the gone?
I have no answers for my children,
I am but pen and ink and tear;
the shadows and the constants
affect those I hold too near.
I only wish to see, before it too disappears,
that which is born but not yet created;
that which lives alone in fear.

Instruction

Everything I have to say has a clear beginning, middle and end.

Beginnings are always hard because a rapport has to be established,
where none before existed: the foundation of trust, of support,
of mutual understanding has to be created, yet when all the two
of us have are sidelong glances and scared but potent imaginations,
think of all the things that can go wrong in those first few seconds
of contact.

The middle is basically an exercise in calm, cool, educated patience.
It's a waiting game, where the one who strikes first always loses;
where silence is no crime, indeed, it's the only weapon of choice;
where I might bruise you if I just so much as flick my eyelid when
you least expect it. It's a torture chamber confined to these four walls;
an execution cell in which I might say yes, but you also may very well
say no: it's a sketch, a shtick, a ménage.

And then of course, the curtain inevitably falls, intact as it must. It
does matter if the audience is standing, and if you've kept their
attention (and your skin) long enough to merit a reprise. You have to
be vicious, but not soulless; brave, but not pedestrian; vague,
but not prosaic. You have to strike the drum, but not break it with
your efforts. The entire performance has to end, but not without it
seeming like it cost you an iota of fear.

There now, that's sophistry.

Not Today

Take this proem
Take this throng
Abuse my meaning
Kill this gong

See if I care, if your
sentiments are in vain;
I've known, always,
that to reject was to gain

an ally, a brother-in-arms,
a field marshal, a woman's charms;
just not today, not here,
not while the customers watch;
they pay to be served --
you pray to be caught

in one of their fishnets.

When The Ether Becomes Viscous

When the ether becomes viscous
Then the dawn takes sway

When the certainty's been questioned
Then I wake to the day

When the meditation's hastened
Then the truth's been betrayed

When the inner light's constricted
Then in this world we pray

When with my love I've mated
Then for breakfast we may

When the gold's been accounted
Then the parties can play

When the rainbow's been whitewashed
Then the horses will neigh

When the ring's been paid for
Then your hand may be claimed

For A Brief Second, The Trauma Recedes

For a brief second, the trauma
      recedes, and I realize: I'm not ill.
Whatever was once, was once before;
      there's no more me, they're trying to kill.
I'm safe here now, in this blue lagoon,
      my therapist wants me no ill —
When I wake and again, the bed feels warm,
      the past here degrades at will.

The conclusion's foregone, to my deep surprise,
      the sickness wants me to kill;
The friends and the family that I've left it despite
      continue to want me all ill;
I imagine their noses and their faces upturned
      as they secretly select their kill:
All I want them to do is to live and let live,
      to leave me alone with my will.

And yet once again the trauma removes and I
      see all alone: I'm ill;
The dreams and the thoughts and murderous
      Gods are all in my brain to kill;
I breathe and remove from their exactitude
      all figment of currency and ill:
Once again I am suddenly bereft of my throne,
      but at least I've found my will.

Then I learn that the shouting's not here anymore,
       that those people long ago claimed their kill;
I wake and to my complete and utter surprise,
       my lover bears me no ill;
I rock her, I bathe her, we go walking together,
       there's no more me she's trying to kill;
As we step, then I realize my life isn't over,
       only now is it starting to will.

This Is How It's Gonna Be

You're gonna sit here and count these numbers. Then, when we tell you to stop, you'll take your 15-minute murder break. After that, you'll count the numbers again, but backwards this time, paying attention to the xenophobia. After *that*, lunch will happen. We're ordering take-out. Hope you like deep-fried vegan zucchini chips. They're good for your heart. You'll spend the afternoon with Sal and me and the boys and we'll explain to Glenn upstairs why our numbers are better than theirs. Finally, we'll decide which number gets to go. If it's not yours, you get to come back tomorrow and do it all over again.

Mother, Mother

Mother, Mother, far below —
on your graveyard, let it snow.
Let those who breathe there, understand:
you love them more, you love them grand.

Mother, Mother, help me sleep —
help me love, those friends I keep.

Mother, Mother, help us go —
ask us not, what we don't know.
Help us see, the gentle strand
your love extends throughout the land.

Mother, Mother, help us weep —
help us share your secrets deep.

14

Heal, Heal My People

Heal, heal my people,
in the morning you'll be free.
Your naked heart will crimson,
the love of she and he.

Hear, hear my people:
you've suffered long enough.
In your soul rekindle
the flame they almost snuffed.

I know you've been deported,
of your culture, deprived;
your villages, extorted;
your babies burned alive.

I've heard your women screaming;
I've seen the guns and wounds;
I know your men, they dug ditches,
while your women were prostitutes.

I see you battle daily
with the anatomy of death;
the sacredness of orphans
is that there's nearly no one left.

Still:

Heal, heal my people,
in the morning you'll be free.
Your naked heart will crimson,
the love of she and he.

Hear, hear my people:
you've suffered long enough.
In your soul rekindle
the flame they almost snuffed.

You argue and you demur:
you mean, we should forget?
Our killers are still nimble;
their boots might hurt us yet.

We want, we need our stories,
of dearth, of darkness and of woe.
With what right do you deprive us
of those memories of long ago?

I make no claim of forgetting,
but forgiveness, too, is sparse;
and so is love, and human caring,
and acceptance and common trust.

So:

Heal, heal my people,
in the morning you'll be free.
Your naked heart will crimson,
the love of she and he.

Hear, hear my people:
you've suffered long enough.
In your soul rekindle
the flame they almost snuffed.

Result Of The Blood Test

There's nothing at all the matter with me. These stories are
just figments of my imagination. The sun is shining and
I can go home now.

Grandma's Way

Grandma had a way
of getting her jokes quite right:
there were always more Nazis
than libertarians;
more Communists than pigs;
she had a way of making
history
seem like so many broken
twigs.

I especially liked the one
with the Germans in the barn;
they would rape and pillage
for hours —
but in the end somehow, the
Jews had always won.

Oh Grandma dear,
how I miss your sense of fun —
your shameless idiosyncrasies;
your selfless stories of guns.

They killed so many of us —
you got tired of the abuse;
and yet, when you laughed,
we understood:
war is never so obtuse
as to lack a sense of humour.

We're Not Looking

We're not looking for recruits,
the movement is behind;
the revolution's over,
but we've an axe to grind.

It's converts that we want,
pure, and worry-free:
melt your soul and wallet—
gain: immortality.

Buy your way to heaven,
earn your midnight loft:
nothing is forbidden,
suppress your gilded cough.

It's only space we're offering,
the mortgage is no-fee;
the petunias are scentless,
we've engineered them for Thee.

You think we need your guilt?
You ideas so abstruse?
Your longing gaze? Your honour?
Your honesty? Your muse?

We've so much better
than anything you propose!
Shed your outworn shoelaces—
sell us your last prose!

Credo

When I said, I wanted freedom,
I wasn't sure of the extent;
turns out, it's not that simple:
power's not what I meant.

I'm learning the art of balance,
of purpose, and of aim;
now, I live in moments,
when before I played the game.

I've sabotaged your theses,
I've lied and I've had enough:
between mud and bricks and feces,
the going has been rough.

I'm embracing all the colours,
all the flesh and all the sin:
I'm helping all the babies
soothe their mothers' skin.

I'm shifting all the stories,
expiating your old crimes,
your sickness and your blastocysts,
and your outworn paradigms.

My Inner Jew

If I exile him, he returns, dejected,
dragging his *tallis*.
He begs me to say Kaddish for my forebears;
to give *tzedakah*; to kneel on Yom Kippur.

If I resist, he becomes angry:
he knows how to spoil my day with
a good guilt-trip.

He is an important part of me,
but if I subscribe to chosenness,
I am a bigot.

With a leap of faith that dares stare
history in the eye:
I choose to love.

Learning To Love

To listen is to learn;
to learn, is to live;
to live, is to heal;
and to heal, is to give.

My Inner Wicked

You know that place, between thinking and dreaming? That's where
my Inner Wicked resides. I do everything to be with my Inner
Wicked. On my daily visits I bring her a copy of the daily schizoid,
and a bullet of violets. She thinks I'm God's gift to humanity.
I call her names, too, but different ones, like: 'nipples'. She humours
me: she once told me I'd be the next Holy Roman Emperor. But
mostly, she tells me: you foolish sap. You don't work nearly hard
enough for your daily three groschen. And you want to go into sales?
I tell her I have no friends. She says — when's the last time you called?
Stop whining and get off your rear. And I do. As I rise, I slowly lower
the toilet seat.

Freezer

Eternal, silent, unmoving,
like the Rockies
I'm the only one who doesn't change.

My friends all have babies now;
their families are secure;
they've wed and bred and satisfied:

my trauma keeps me pure.

22

Education

I first heard the words
'gas chamber' when I was nine.

It was in a small room at summer camp in the
Laurentians.

A dark room
full of black and white photographs of children
like me —

but dying, or waiting to do so.

We had many sessions in that room.

Randy, our counselor, would show us maps of the
death marches on our free
Saturday afternoons in August.

The need for memory and the hunger to forget had
never been so juxtaposed as in those moments in the dark —

while the other Canadian kids played Frisbee outside.

Some Jews

Some Jews I know
are the most resilient people ever;
the most traumatized;
and the most alone.

Please —
give them of the
generosity of
your love.

Thaw

Slowly, the old rivulets remember:
we, too, once a'-used to be.
Before our glacial terms of surrender,
we wandered these meadows with Thee.

You were not afraid back then—
and witnessed past was not time lost.
You dared to look and be forgiven,
to listen again and at no cost.

Trust again, yourself, without asking,
to give your muse her share of support;
to love; to live; to fulfill without masking;
the pain you've endured only adds to your growth.

Beagles, California

Men in the cancer of poésum were
walking alone, bereft of any
fiction of living, their only
consolation a line or two at the expense
of a singular, *fleshy* experience.

"There is no war," they insisted, while outside,
women were violated with machetes
and children were hanged.

Tree Of My Hate

Implicitly, of course – nothing
was ever stated, we were all
Kosher in that regard – but
I grew up hating, without
ever knowing it. Multiculturalism
was a 'sham'. As far as I remember,
in the Montreal of the 90s, everyone
just hung out with their own.

I Wish I Could Love

I'm facing bereavement, refugee-dom and blame;
give me something rancid, help me kill the pain.
There's a tear in the fabric, a rip in the cloth:
the pain, it is plastic, the handling's been rough.

I came here unbidden, at the lowly age of five.
My whole world was shaken when I was circumcised.
My mother's a poet, my father's a scribe;
my sisters are prophets: am I still alive?

I came to curry pleasure, I seek to ease the pain.
There's no corpse I can't measure; feed me to the flame.
There's a fear in the music, a tear in the cloth.
A dog in the alley: *how I wish I could love.*

I wish I could love.

Jonah's Answer

True, there's a fear in the fabric,
and the rip on my groin isn't new.
And yet, when they ask,
  'what now?' and
  'what after?'
I live in the moment, like you.

I'd rather not know, what the morrow will bring,
and when the night comes to die on your lawn,
I'd rather hope, than expect, and feel worthless;
I'd rather believe than be pawned.

For, scared am I too, and pain notwithstanding,
the years haven't obscured my faith;
its depth and its volume have shifted but lately,
though presence is all that love takes.

Not that I'm angry, nor weary, nor fractured,
I just keep to my own, and brew:
bereft of the truth that youth breathes, as it flowers,
I bring all my flowers, to you.

Adjectives

Today, you're a strong, white male. You have responsibilities; you run a business and write cheques. You speak good English and everyone wants lessons with you.

And yet two days ago, you were but a wicked Anglophone, who spoke the wrong language and who by his very being threatened the entire political establishment.

And before that, still, you were racially and ethnically circumscribed: a dirty little Jew, a filthy miscreant on whom all kinds of calamities could be blamed, at will.

So how are you supposed to impress me with your grammar? Are you surprised that I find no solace in your rhetoric? Must I not shun your debilitating pieces of paper, and vegetate while the ink dries?

It's all the same, really. Tomorrow, you might decide that I'm worthy of torture; a fortnight hence, you just might ask me to patriotically assent to my own execution. The funny thing is, we both know I will.

It's our destiny.

The Evil Within

Every time I decide to not give charity; every time I look askance when you ask me for help; every time I shrug when you say you're sorry; that's when the real killing begins. Your bones don't belong to you; this tongue isn't mine, either. But the joy I get when I set you aflame – it's unparalleled. When you wince, I get a rush of pride. The more intricate the layers, the more passionate (say: dangerous) the game; the more we suffer; the more we are entangled. And yet then I step back; breathe and collect myself; and you and I are God's children again, playing a silly game of checkers. Is it any wonder, then, that we find it so hard to stop?

Eastern Europe

Look at you –
squabbling over long-lost territories like toddlers
grabbing toys at the playground.

You all think that the guy next door has it better;
that your language and so-called national potpourri
are more worthy of statues and minarets than the
other person's.

You cry that the West didn't help you back in 19--;
that those German and Russian tanks that felled your fields
were everyone else's fault, but not also your own.

Tell me again, what happened to those Yiddish-speakers
who used to live in your midst? Those same ones who,
two centuries ago, established sugar factories and
railroads? They're still there, you know –

just in a different form, haunting your conscience,
while you bicker and moan and pick on the Gypsies.
And the other immigrants.

I'm Not In The Business Of Pleasing You Anymore

I've shuttered the windows; I've closed the store;
the last customers have walked out; there's
"space available" on the door.

As businesses go, it was quite a successful run.
Years of put-downs, of guilt trips, of "I did this for you"
and the periodic insults – I know you don't do it on purpose –
it's part of your chemise, you're just a negative person,
after all.

And yet, you did it remorselessly, without questioning,
hammering away at the nails; feeding me, clothing me,
helping me be exactly in your image: a twisted, soulless
cynic.

They say that the road to hell is paved with good intentions –
honey, let me tell you, this one's as shiny as the Mona Lisa;
as mysterious – as deadly.

So You Wanna Go To College

Well, let me tell you –
        it ain't what it used to be.

You have to start early, and I mean, at the age of diapers,
not pencil sharpeners. Yo Moma better start savin' up
her cents; Daddy's gone work ovatime.

Better start suckin' up to teachers; coaches; bosses; gotta
get 'dem letters of rec. An' start usin' your friends, too: they'll
be useful business acolytes.

Learn to score better than the machine your answers get fed to:
one day, you'll feed it too.

Forget soccer practice.

If you've a disparity, or green skin, please tell us: but gently,
so as not to offend our sensibilities. We'll hook you up with our
employee discount.

What was that about grades? Well, if you have to ask, you'd better not
apply here. You're not our type of success, anyway.

We want malleable souls; individuality in the name of conformity;
open wallets.

Nobody cares if you took six AP courses, or two.

Will you still love me, tomorrow?

So, You Wanna Teach College?

Oh ho – ho ho ho ho ho ho ho ho ho – wait, please, a second –
I have to catch my breath. I'm sixty, you know, and I have white man's
angina – oh, you're still here?

Well, we have no positions. If you want to teach remedial English,
you can, and it pays (let me check) I think fifteen cents an hour?
Kinda like what we paid Mark Twain, when he started out
on the Mississippi.

I'll put you down on our list of sub-alternates; let me know if they
call you.

I hope that's OK. We're really tight on funds. I mean, Prof. Good-
enough is on Sabbatical and Prof. Gorgias is on research in Crete.
Actually, here, won't you buy their latest book?

Recent Thoughts About My Religion

The *shul* is broke.

Nobody wants to come listen anymore, to how we're better than the *goyim*.

Intermarriage is at an all-time high!

A full fifty-eight percent of young daughters and sons of Israel have decided they'd rather walk their dog, instead of their dogma.

They have no idea how much this betrayal hurts those who pretend to care.

Self-Introduction

I am just a Jew,
like you.

I wear your clothes.

We May Be Humans, Yet

In this epoch of the abyss; in
these factories of doom; in these
mountains we've conquered; in this
karaoke of gloom –

Whoso begat the poet? Whereto
justice, its claim? Wherefrom passion,
its freedom? Must we really be the
same?

Distill your tempered solders! Refuse
the mark of death! Confuse your angels,
their mercy! We may be humans,
yet.

Kóhn

It's 1938 and the emigration office is full of pauperized men with
their hats in their hands, ready to leave. Their families are all in tow:
Goldie, with her orb, is playing on the parquet; Fruma reads a carol
with Hana. Kóhn is up there, heaving to and fro in front of the bald,
overweight, unshaven bureaucrat with the tweed jacked; they are
having one last go at the plea bargain.
'I told you, you could go to Australia, but the visa requirements are
that you be single – '
'Ah – '
'Or you could try Denmark, I hear they like intellectuals like you.'
'Oh – '
The functionary adjusts his metal nose clips and looks up, non-
plussed, from the sheaves of paper, one for each family member.
'Tell me,' says Kóhn at length, but softly, his voice the sound of
molten ash, 'is there no other Earth?'

– *after my father.*

And Are You Really That Smart?

And are you really that smart?
So much better than people without feelings,
whom you denigrate and mock at every turn of the screw?

And that much more worthy, so ever well-connected,
than those who toil with their hands;
those who share your stool?

Is it ever a pressing issue, to deserve a lack of ambition,
to force a sedge between a lamb and her ewe?
To open heart and viscera, so painful and grotesque,
to the added scorn of those deep in muck and goop?

Breathe, dear child, Thou starling of the ages;
Thy plastered face is not the one the crowds will hear.
Rejoice in the emblem of your sufferings; advance God's purpose
with those to whom you live so near.

We're Not Animals

Precisely when this happened, I'm not sure.

Death Is An Image

Death is an image:
it's my picture of you dressing down;
it's your cured dentelle;
it's your chemise and your gown.

Death is a mirage:
it's your infatuation at noon;
it's my twisted perspective;
it's our gilded honey-room.

Death is so vintage:
the eldest are to blame –
the culprits, they're endless;
the ceremony, so lame.

Death is so sexless:
so joyless, it's a crime;
there's no talk of loving;
your body's at its prime.

To Our Drug Addiction

Your syringes, too, they're useless; it's with
phenylethols that we kiss; your troubadours
are careless; theirs is the pathos of your bliss.

Paradox Of The Age

The motif is: eat and be merry.
And yet my tradition says: work for the benefit of all.

The concept is: earn as much dough as possible in a day.
My conscience says: rest on the Sabbath.

The creed is: let's all be intersexed, and let's all intermarry.
My upbringing cries: don't take a wife from amongst the Canaanites!
(And sodomy is sin.)

Would that it were so simple that I could fully side with one, or the
other.

Teacher's College

When ye have been taught how to teach,
you will whisper, each to each –
"We have been licensed to preach –
not earn, but to screech."

History Of The World (Except Not Racist)

You write such great poetry.
Must you also be an anti-Semite?

Some

Some go in for hunger; I'm blessed to have always been eaten.
Some do it out of wonder; in your garden, I got beaten.
Some confiscate; some groom; some vegetate uneven.
Some do it in the road; some demonstrate they're heathen.
Some are worthy; some are creakin'; some communicate their beacon.
Some gesticulate; some constipate; some usurp and are browbeaten.

Pomegranate

Every time I cut you open –
    I feel like I'm committing murder in the first degree.
Every time I bite and your flesh reduces –
    I remember when I was touched, inappropriately.
When I scoop up the stragglers from your once-mighty kingdom,
    I massacre your innocents with impunity.
But when I gaze down at your sun-soaked cathedral,
    I am chagrined to know, why the profound mingle with profanity.

You, Who Feel So Threatened

You, who feel so threatened;
you, who feel so cruel:
begrudge not, your servants, your sinew;
give blessings and alms to the poor.

Accept the millions, their curses;
murder not in the wake of shame;
caress neither the grafted skin asunder;
heal the wicked with balms of praise.

Most important, ye patron saints,
understand that your time too, will come;
when fashion reeks and stores portend,
what cometh then is dark offal.

Seek not pleasure, its glaze;
worry not that your tale will bend;
bury your treasures and in sackcloth mend,
your ways of measure, your days of Lent.

Wordsworth

I wondered lonely as a crowd:
"Who floats on high over dale and hill?"
When all at once I saw a cloud –
A host! A golden daffodil!

When oft upon my couch I lie,
in vacant but in pensive mood,
mist obscures that inward eye,
which is the bliss of solicitude.

And then my bowl with pleasure fills;
I dance with all my daffodils.

Fact vs Fiction

Power is fact; the fiction comes next. First we establish the
currency; then, we see what's left. Upon your word, you will not
mention, what you saw or heard transgress; to be sure, we'll have
notified, all authorities, if you egress. Your position is to repeat,
all you've said under duress; your services shall not cease; we'll only
intensify our caress. You will pretend like you weren't emasculated;
like you've only acquired finesse. But you'll know, deep down,
that we've won: your skill, we will possess.

Exhibit: Zoological

Pigeon

You're born dirty,
fluttering in that gutter:
otherwise, I'd eat you.

Frogs

Crabbing and croaking,
crafting and crowing,
from some other degenerative disease;
planning and knowing,
harping and moaning,
you poison the mud and its fleas.

Digits

I met this young woman, it was a blind date.
She said – your skill and your service,
doubtless, I can appreciate.
So I asked, what's the problem? She said:
it's not you, it's mine! Your digits are thirty,
and my number's five-oh-nine.

The State Of The Fridge At 11 PM

They say that famine breeds
ineptitude and sullenness,
and also that gluttony is bliss.

Every time I examine the foodshelf,
I am reminded of that primordial urge
to simply not go hungry.

Sure, I mean, it's all fine and good
until we run out of food – and then,
are we all supposed to eat one another?

Would *you* kill for your next meal?
I mean, we *did* use to do that, remember?
Aeons ago, when mammoths patrolled
the Plains of Abraham.

So, how *civilized* are we, really?
Could we do without hunger?
Fame? Prostitution?

Must we celebrate brokenness?
Or rather, the fact that our streets are paved
and that there is (still) gold in the mine?

I'm not so sure. All I can tell you is that sometimes,
I don't know where the next meal will come from;
but that I am always grateful.

It's Time To Go Teach Again

Time to wrap up the self-pity and look semi-presentable.
At least for this afternoon, let's pretend that scansion is easy.
They say that this profession is for those who like to take time off;
those (like me) who enjoy cutting corners; those, still, who aspire to a
minimal sense of social relevance but lack the necessary impetus for
true worldly success. Nothing could be farther from the truth.
We teach because the children have no choice but to listen to us, and
the adults, they know better...

The Moment

The moment that I accept responsibility for whom I am becoming; when I understand that the pain you inflicted was neither my merit but clearly your sin; that's when you start to unravel. Because that's when I fully cross the threshold into Being. Until then, I am victimized; meaningless, worthless putty in your hands. But the moment I now say – stop! – you become nothing for me. I outgrow the pain you inflicted. I flower; I merge into love again; this time, without you. I take ownership of this life I have been offered; I no longer complain of being alone because I have assumed control. You are neither here nor there, now; my resources are not limitless (i.e., it still hurts to walk); but I have detached; I have moved on. It was so easy for you: making me feel like I was somehow flawed inside. Somehow not quite right. And there you have it: *you* were the problem all along! You resented responsibility – I welcome it. You succumbed – I say, enough.

The moment I realize this, is the moment that you stop mattering; the moment you become just another amongst God's creations; rotten a bit, it is true, on the inside, but in effect, quite harmless. I would accost you; give you the opportunity to redeem yourself; to volunteer your sadness, your inability, for mine. I know you too well: you would rebuff any sense of finality that I would gain. So the way to let you go is with a shrug. I am in control now. I would never hit a child; I remember the stench of the alcohol that subsumed you, then; it's not my fault if you don't fit into my value system. You did what you had to do. It's outrageous. But your finesse at denying is only more so. Anger uses up creative energy; choosing to distance myself is glory and peace.

The Way They Get To You

The way they get to you is by making you believe that their remonstrances and recriminations are essential ingredients to your health. But that isn't so. You don't need the pallor; think of the emptiness and valor you find when you move away and realize: they themselves are powerless against the inner constants. Those parallel eternities, you take them for granted! They will come to you, with words this time: isn't it time you bought a house? Little do they know that you have no use for such chains; and that the momentary attachment they oblige to such worldly phenomena is transparent and fictitious.

Yes, but you have to eat! Yes, I reply, and I do! There are figs, and mint leaves, and olives on my table. The urgency of their tone belies their lack of trust. And what about the future? Think about that! And you know what I say then? Twenty years ago, you said the same thing, and you were no happier. So, yes: what about the future? The future is now. That's what the con men, the insurance people want to make you forget. The instant that that this very moment becomes meaningful to you: that's when you radically defeat any sense of powerlessness that the other party wants to impose. When we get married, we will – when we retire, we will – when this bond matures, it will – . Instead: when the time comes, you will get married; you will retire; it will mature. Now is not that time. Enjoy it. Go dancing.

Football

When she spoke about athletes, my Grandma used to quote the
Hungarian humorist Karinthy: "If he wants the ball, why does he kick
it away? And if he has no use for it, why does he give it chase?" In
effect, she was dissertating on the transience of suffering.
Soon, they will kick someone else and they will let you recover in the
shed. And then, when you have known enough thuggery, you will not
kick others. Until you do; at which point, you will become others'
sport again. And my Grandma just laughed and laughed…

I Used To Say

I used to say: to hell with this senseless, degraded religion; we are all
just parasites and anyway, the *mohel* is a simple functionary.

I've abandoned my family and I've nothing left to lose. So, those reli-
gious hours spent in prepubescent mirth did have a purpose, after all:
I know where to go now, to pray.

Prayer Of The Voiceless

Please father, not today.
I'm two and I'm afraid.
Mother can't protect me.
I know why you do it, too:
you're drunk &
you've no control.
One day, I will exorcise your ghosts,
and you can love me again.
But please, not today, daddy.

We Don't Say No Thank You's

We don't say no thank you's;
no *pass auf* and no *how-do-you-do*'s.
We don't give no 'cknowledgments;
no marzipans, no free shoes.

If you've struggled, so be it;
if you've won, then you're well-off;
if you've molten, if you've bungled:
God be with you; we've shared our trough.

We never asked you come here;
your presence at our communion is, at best, a cough;
you did it without mercy —
if we've left you alone, let that be:

enough.

Stranger

I hope you read this. I can't but somehow remember that we knew each other, long ago. You loved me. You didn't know — weren't exposed to — the evil that works in men's hearts. Nature spared you that way. You only saw his good side — his charisma, his nonchalance, his ease at bringing plates to the table. How then can you believe me, that I had to do, what I had to do? That, to be whole again, I had to break the rusty cantilever; to remove myself from the site of my own sacrifice?

All I am sorry for is that sometimes, the wheat must go with the chaff; sometimes, the bathwater suffocates the baby. I miss you; you loved me. You gave me your records.

I Want You To Love Me, The Way I Want You To Love Me

Not with your ambitions for me;
not with your insistence, that everything be interpreted;
some things, they just *are*.

I want you to love me — if you can — like you love the air,
or the beating sound in your eardrums
when the pressure changes.

I want you to love me, like the pebble in your pocket:
soft, inconspicuous, slightly maladroit,
eminently graceless.

I want you to love me like some forgotten ship,
that has sailed away with all its cargo lost.

I want you to love me
without thinking of the consequences.

My Body Still Remembers

My body still remembers
the frozen waltz of time:
your rings instead were embers;
your fingers, they were nine.

My body still remembers
my penumbral sense of shame;
the solitude of mercy;
your rancid stench of pain.

My body still remembers
the protean shriek of death;
the degeneracy of escape;
how in the morning, you'd defect.

My body still remembers,
but my mind, it soon forgets;
and shields itself with torpor,
with hallucinations and regrets.

Charity Like Crystal

In order to trick the prisoners into thinking that they would be getting a reprieve, the guards told them that in the evening they would be receiving acacia honey with their coffees. The condemned were excited. All but one had a sweet tooth, and honey was considered an extravagance. To receive their gifts, they lined up at the appointed hour in front of the commissary. Only the honey seemed so — vitreous; the coffee — so much like gelatin. A couple of the unlucky ones tried the dubious-looking compote; it was clear that they would not survive the night. Would you, had you noticed that you were gulping down the cellblock's molten windowpanes?

The Poetry Of Evil

Surprisingly, but it has no real cadences; no metonymy; no dispersals of meaning and allegory; no abstract rectifications; no existence beyond itself. It's more like a massacre; a cascade of dung; the clattering of metal in the tool shed, before the execution. The pain it tries to transpose is voiceless; the rules it obeys are those of gratuitous terror and sadistic barbarism. Why then are we so attracted to its sickening, inhuman wordings? Because as plebeians, we find fascination in suffering; and reassurance in the fact that for once, it's not our very own.

They Will Buy

They w'll buy you in Nyu Yoark Siddi
They will buy you and make you pretty
They'll buy you at the Taj Mahal
They will buy you at the Berlin Wall

They'll buy you at the Mardi Gras
They we'll buy you when they make a faux-pas
They will buy you in Victory Square
They'll buy you with Molière

Day will buy you at the Red River Delta
They'll buy you with their favorite pizza
They'll buy you at Kafka's grave
They will bah you like a Roman slave

They will buy you with a crooked nose
They will bye your bag of bones
They'll buy you at the Bight of Biafra
They well buy you in Togo and Botswana

Thejl bayou in Gibraltar
They will buy you near the altar
Theil buy you by the door
They will buy your ancient lore.

They will buy you up in 'Aza
They will buy you down in Giza
They will buy you with the wooden chair
They will buy you, when you weren't even there.

Author's Note

To what has been set down, there is paltry little to add. The heart grieves daily for that, which has been lost; it hopes and yearns for that, which may yet come. I feel lucky to have benefitted from a series of environments in Budapest, Montreal, Fukui City, and Berkeley, where, despite everything else, the twin pursuits of letters and of spirituality were seen as positive goods. I am grateful to my teachers, who tried to show me the ways of words. I hope that in my quest for authenticity, I have not alienated those for whom these poems might mean the most.

There was no creative process, taken in the usual sense. As I struggled with depression, anxiety, death, and post-traumatic stress disorder, I heard the words, and I wrote them down. Sometimes, I rearranged the lines and found a better synonym or two; on the whole, though, the poems just came. The words wanted to be preserved. I hope the result is meaningful.

That is all.

Vancouver, British Columbia
April 2018

CPSIA information can be obtained
at www.ICGtesting.com
Printed in the USA
FSHW021900011220
76486FS